Inside the Invisible

Daniel Simpson

To my mother, Miriam Dell
and my wife, Ona Gritz

NINE MILE BOOKS
PROPEL DISABILITY POETRY SERIES

WINNER PROPEL POETRY AWARD

Publisher: Nine Mile Art Corp.
Editors: Stephen Kuusisto, Andrea Scarpino
Front Cover Art: Wendy Setzer, "Cherry Blossoms in the Sun," 2022, monotype print, 14"x20¼"

Nine Mile Books is an imprint of Nine Mile Art Corp.

The publishers gratefully acknowledge support of the New York State Council on the Arts with the support of the Governor and the New York State Legislature. We also acknowledge support of the County of Onondaga and CNY Arts through the Tier Three Project Support Grant Program. This publication would not have been possible without the generous support of these groups. We are very grateful to them all.

ISBN: 979-8-9871927-6-4

Table of Contents

Introduction

I've always favored poets who've had musical educations. Dan Simpson is both a classically trained musician as well as a poet. Reading his work I'm reminded of Pope's observation: *Music resembles poetry, in each/Are nameless graces which no methods teach,/And which a master hand alone can reach.*

Consider the opening of his poem "Some Holy Saturday":

You will rise from your bed at four-thirty in the morning,
to find bitter weeping outside your window
and your yard filled with trees that were not there the night
    before,
large leaves everywhere soaking your hair with dew,
the thick smell of olives heavy in the air.
It is Peter, still crying
up through the crust of the earth,
and though no cocks have crowed yet,
and there is no farm for hours,
you are poised for the marking of betrayal.

It is Peter, still crying/up through the crust of the earth— spondee and dactyl mixing it up and behind them the oboe of the traduced heart. This is music in the service of spirit and while most of us cannot reach it, a master hand just might, especially if the poet who's blind and thinking of Christ's betrayal is walking the verse into being:

What will you do
if, following Leopard Road or Route 13,
you should be drawn by a congregation of curious crows
to Iscariot hanging from a tree,
the neck groove lapping over the rope,
his toga tented at the crotch?
And what if from the moon come strains
of Hollywood's fourth cousin to Gregorian chant

with celluloid clicks and pops to let you know
this is old and serious?

This is a sober poem, a tone poem as Sibelius would have it, and for all its music the verse turns toward mentation and discovery:

> *And what if the man who made the cross*
> *sleepwalks beside the road in the underbrush,*
> *and your father now remembers*
> *that yesterday, between twelve and three,*
> *the sky grew dark over your neighborhood?*
> *Will you kneel down in the road and pray?*
> *Run to your home to take from your kitchen cinnamon and*
>   *nutmeg,*
> *the only spices appropriate for the Savior's tomb?*
> *Call the police?*
> *Or walk to your church in silence,*
> *hoping that the sun upon your back*
> *is really the large hand of the fisherman reconciled?*

I think here of Benjamin Britten who said of music: "It has the beauty of loneliness of pain: of strength and freedom. The beauty of disappointment and never-satisfied love. The cruel beauty of nature and everlasting beauty of monotony."

Simpson's poems propose that musicality should strive toward making sense—of losses, of small or large discoveries, of the very business of inquiry. There is even comedy in this as the poet meditates on what takes the place of literature in the lives of those who don't read it:

> *Let us pray for poetry*
> *that begins in love*
> *and then moves outward.*
> *May it fill the mouths*
> *of all who love.*

"My dancing tumbleweed,"
the crane operator will say
to his wife on a Sunday walk.
And the bookstore clerk, leaving for work,
will embrace her beloved in the kitchen.
"Oh, my hot skillet," she will say,
"my deep, deep fryer."

Lawrence said he preferred his heart to be broken: "It is so lovely, dawn-kaleidoscopic within the crack." Simpson asks us to conceive of our limitations as evocative and darkly comedic matters:

Schoenberg

Why would a young dog
give itself to guide the blind?
Ask the right question
to get a useful answer.
Did the dog have a choice?

What did the dog do,
once they neutered it
and slammed the kennel door
on its freedom dream?
It did its best to flourish.

And what about you—what
choices do you have left?
Do you take pleasure,
as Schoenberg did in twelve tones,
unleashed by your limitations?

These are poems of advantageous doubt and they are rich and lyrical and invite us to take pleasure. The latter is aesthetically subversive given the public's longstanding view of blindness— that it's a profound limitation that goes beyond sightlessness to suggest a blunted capacity for knowledge. When a blind poet invites readers to unleash their own limitations via the challenge of pleasure, one realizes how few analogies are to be found in the work of whatever we mean by "non-disabled" poets.

Inside the Invisible is the 2022 winner of the Propel Poetry Award. The award celebrates a book-length collection of poems by a crip/disabled poet at any career stage.

We are very grateful to Jeremy Mindich, co-founder of Propel, and his team, who have made this series possible. Propel is a philanthropic fund dedicated to building a world where everyone has a chance to thrive. Propel's focus also includes reimagining a democracy and economy that work for the many, investing in early-stage ventures and visionary leaders challenging the status quo and driving transformational change.

—Stephen Kuusisto

Part One

A Blind Boy's First Glimpse of Heaven

I climbed the stepladder to Heaven when I was eight,
my father spotting me from behind.
I liked that he stayed below.
How else could I hear where the world was?

"You can move around, Son, but shuffle your feet,
in case there's a stray bale of hay to trip over,
and you don't want to walk off the edge."

God was in a meeting, I guess.
Anyway, I never saw Him.
What had He done to Lucifer?
And what did the Bible mean by "cast him out?"

Did God have a squad of angel goons up there
to blind-side him from the back and shove him off?
I wanted to jump, to see if I'd survive.

Fifty years later, Aunt Polly said,
"You better get ready, Dan, if you want God
to take you up to be with your Dad again,
and won't it be great to finally see his face?"

I don't know. I'm just getting to love
this world for what it is, a flawed place
with its subway platforms overlooking the third rail,
its open sewers, loading docks, and construction sites
and all the strangers who've looked out for me,
letting me take their arms to walk with them.

I'm thinking, the next time I see Aunt Polly,
I'm going to tell her about my new vision.
"It's really going to be something," I'll say.
"In Heaven, you'll finally get to be blind."

Some Holy Saturday

you will rise from your bed at four-thirty in the morning,
to find bitter weeping outside your window
and your yard filled with trees that were not there the night
    before,
large leaves everywhere soaking your hair with dew,
the thick smell of olives heavy in the air.
It is Peter, still crying
up through the crust of the earth,
and though no cocks have crowed yet,
and there is no farm for hours,
you are poised for the marking of betrayal.
What will you do
if, following Leopard Road or Route 13,
you should be drawn by a congregation of curious crows
to Iscariot hanging from a tree,
the neck groove lapping over the rope,
his toga tented at the crotch?
And what if from the moon come strains
of Hollywood's fourth cousin to Gregorian chant
with celluloid clicks and pops to let you know
this is old and serious?
And what if the man who made the cross
sleepwalks beside the road in the underbrush,
and your father now remembers
that yesterday, between twelve and three,
the sky grew dark over your neighborhood?
Will you kneel down in the road and pray?
Run to your home to take from your kitchen cinnamon and
    nutmeg,
the only spices appropriate for the Savior's tomb?
Call the police?
Or walk to your church in silence,
hoping that the sun upon your back
is really the large hand of the fisherman reconciled?

Why Shouldn't I?

Why shouldn't I believe that Lazarus,
moldering in the grave, crawled up and out,
alive and fresh when called forth by Jesus,
or that Jesus could zoom through a locked door
to appear to his followers and let Thomas touch him?
And if I could believe those stories, I asked myself,
what could be so hard about the virgin birth?
My father said he believed in all of it,
and I feared I would be wandering in a desert
without a pillar of cloud to guide me
if I didn't find ways to believe what he believed.
And never did I want to more than when
a girl I thought I'd never hold told me
I'd have to believe if I wanted her to stay.
(Her breast rested on my arm as she said this.)
Couldn't it be enough, I asked her, if
I aimed to live a life of never taking
for granted the mouse, the butterfly, the snoring dog?
As for Lazarus, isn't it enough
to think it a miracle that he got here,
like the rest of us, through the blending of sperm and egg?
If only I could imagine that anything is possible!
But I saw my father, smart in the way of men
who work with their hands and rely on common sense,
swindled by slick salesmen's promises,
like the one of the super-sensitive smoke alarm
"guaranteed for life and loud enough to wake the dead."
Three nights in a row, we ran into the street
in our pajamas because gnats or dust had set it off.
(The company's whereabouts could not be traced.)
So how then shall I live inside the invisible?
There is no Jesus here for me to touch,
unless it is you, wearing his disguise.

Father's Day

No card to send, nowhere to send one,
I remember the concierge telling me
on my way out the door to call home soon.
Afraid of bad news, I went first to Notre Dame
to hear a man missing fingers send up mystical prayers
to the Holy Spirit through ten thousand pipes.
"I'm a tough timber to crack," you said after "cancer,"
your voice strong and sure via satellite.
But you did crack, leaving me lost but still playing
memories of rituals: backyard baseball,
lunch at the deli, trips to the lumberyard,
slow afternoons on the train station bench,
the devoted waiting for the Spirit of St. Louis,
with her one-chord prelude and her sanctus bell,
to pass through our world with a thousand souls,
sending up diesel like incense, like prayer.

Measuring Distance

They blow the whistle by my house
and a long way down the track.

They don't blow it at yours.
I know that from sitting on your lawn.

The train that lumbers to a start near me
whooshes by the far end of your yard.

Today, I tried to see how long I could hear it.
I was surprised how loud it was so far away—

surprised as when a New York FM station
made me think I was hearing Radio France.

I imagined the train passing by your place;
I can't exactly say when it faded.

What if I called you up some day
and you stood outside with your cordless phone,

perhaps the same one your old boyfriend rang
that broke the spell I had fallen under?

(You were sleeping on a blanket.
I was sitting near you, reading poems.)

Would we be able, together, to subtract
the rails between your home and mine?

Chance Meeting

You are riding on a train,
and since it is such a long trip
and your book is boring,
and since she seems to have nothing to do
but glance out the window
and once or twice at you,
you cautiously tuck your shyness,
like a bookmark,
into the cheap paperback
you bought in the station
at the last minute
and you say something to her.
It isn't much of a thing to say—
something safe—
and yet you feel
as if you are saying
something crucial and awkward
as you did when saying
almost anything in seventh grade.
You scratch your shoulder,
which doesn't itch,
and you say something like
"Boy, Ohio is really flat" or
"I don't know if I could live
in this city" and then

she says something back. It isn't
much of anything either. But maybe,
because you spoke first, or because
she's just that way, she sounds
a little more sure of herself.
And perhaps because the train
clatters along confidently,
you tell each other

where you live and what you do,
and then you both say that you are
hungry and wouldn't mind
walking the eleven cars
to the snack bar. You agree
that it would be good
to stretch your legs.

On the way,
because the train is swaying,
you link arms for support.
When you squeeze past the conductor,
rather than going single file,
you turn toward each other
so that you are fairly dancing,
rocking between aisle seats
as if they were couples too.
And when you lose your balance
and fall into a stranger's lap,
she laughs at you
with that understanding laughter
married people have,
and you laugh with her
as though you haven't laughed
since a year ago November.

By the time you return
to your seats, you are talking
about favorite movies, you are
telling family stories. And soon
you are using words like wish
and imagine, and you imagine
this could go on forever.
Then the conductor is
calling out her stop,
but she hasn't heard him

and so must hurry now
to pull her luggage from a rack
and make her way.
There is only time
to shout your number once.
She says she's got it,
she'll remember it.
You fiddle with your book.
When you look up,
everyone is watching you and smiling.
A young boy several seats away
turns on a boombox
and the car is filled with music.

We All Have Something of the Poet in Us

which is why
the bookstore clerk
passing through aisles
of Danielle Steel
and waiting for new words
has stopped telling her boyfriend
that she loves him

and why the crane operator
who would take the Phillies
over Frost any day
nevertheless searches his mind
before resigning himself to
Sweetheart
Darling
Honey
the names already used up
by previous lovers.

We all want
a new language,
to smell
the musk of sex
for the first time
every time,
to touch the new one's skin
clean of history.

Let us pray for poetry
that begins in love
and then moves outward.
May it fill the mouths
of all who love.

"My dancing tumbleweed,"
the crane operator will say
to his wife on a Sunday walk.
And the bookstore clerk, leaving for
work, will embrace her beloved in the
kitchen. "Oh, my hot skillet," she will say,
"my deep, deep fryer."

Haiku Love

I want to live
haiku relationships—
that rich, that defined—

believing confinement will
save me from myself,
or from the other.

But then I think
of Schoenberg,
how mathematical music

can sound like chaos,
no melody to sing,
and I say,

Give me sprawling love—the kind that refuses to live in
twelve tones and seventeen syllables, or even in a short story—

that is until
my replacement
comes along,

and everything
is blown to hell,
then couldn't we have

a sonnet,
a sestina,
a villanelle?

American Girl and French Boy Take a Walk

The sun is lowering a basket of light
down into the treetops,
and French II seems so far away.

She recalls her favorite word, the one for *grapefruit*.
Je veux manger du pamplemousse,
je l'aime bien, je l'aime beaucoups.

If she said that, could he get past the words,
forget everything he knew,
dive straight into the sound, and live in that?

And of course, she must tell him
everything—some day, at least—
that it also makes her think of *pimply moose*
(every beauty having its own beast).

She makes their arms swing as they walk,
and she thinks, *Pamplemousse*
rhymes with it's no use.

He holds her hand.
So they have that—
the language of touch and silence.

They smile a lot and he tries to talk.
"Shhhh," she whispers,
a word they have in common.

My Pants Are Drenched with Rain

which came sideways and up my legs
as I walked home from the bus.

Once, Jenny filled my hand with hers
as we walked in the drizzle.
Her hands were wide and quiet—
hands that could listen,
quiet like a priest at confession.

My father's hands were busy,
not soft and uncalloused like mine.
I touched all the caskets before I chose
a pine box that was smooth and lean—
no nicks or splinters like the rocking boat
he hammered together for me in the cellar.
I picked a pine box for him, and the sun poured down.

But now, my pants are drenched with rain.
May there be no time this weekend—
no time and not too much sun.
May there be no more train whistles
saying you must go somewhere,
and none of the usual loneliness.

I have other pants, dry pants,
that would match the red shirt with the swan,
the one I have on.

I am rich; my ears are full of talk.
Once, my arms were full of someone half my age.
Her shirt was filling up with water
and yet she breathed air in and out.
She did this repeatedly and without effort.
Everything she did amazed me.

Pretty soon, I will be dry.
Will the memory of my father fade
the way rain evaporates?

My mind is full of words.
I have not run out of things to say.
I make emphatic statements about the future and the present:
"Jesus shall reign" and "the rain it raineth every day."

How many years of rain
make dust of a wooden coffin?

Jenny just called to say
it is raining in Seattle now, too.

Portrait of My Father

Chewer of fingernails,
smoker of Camels,
tenor in the church choir,
not much of a reader,
dead at 53,

he cold-cocked a friend
who rode him too hard at work
but said, when that friend
became suicidal,

"You spend too much time
alone; come over,
have dinner with my family,
just sit around and talk.
You call me when
you get to feeling that way."

Why mention that he whipped me—
belt, paddle, his bare hand?
It was nothing
put up against the braille spinner

he made out in his shed
so I could play board games
with my sighted sisters. Nothing next
to the hours he read to me.

No need to bring up
the time he shook me
till my teeth rattled.
It would only wipe out his whistling in
the kitchen as he stirred my oatmeal.

You should have heard him sing. You
should have seen him dance.

My Mother Cleans

More exacting than graceful,
she does a turn around my kitchen.
The satellite radio plays
"I'll Never Smile Again."
Is she thinking of dancing,
the way he turned her,
the way he turned her head back then,
some sixty years and a death ago?
Between my stove and microwave,
she manages a neat slide,
leading a mop.

Night Journey

They are painting my room.
Raggedy sheets and plastic drop cloths cover
my bed and dresser, the record player.
Fumes fog up from the floor and fill downward
from the ceiling, which leaves me,
a ten-year-old boy to sleep
with my fourteen-year-old sister
in her double bed.

On the porch, she had shown me how
movie star men held their lean-back ladies
as they kissed them full on the lips.
Now she lies on her stomach,
motionless, the soft puffs on her chest
squished into the springy mattress,
the edge of the left puff
not far from my right wrist.

I want to touch her bare foot
with mine, to leave it there, and I do,
with no complaint from her.
I feel a happiness,
a kind of traveling.
Down the hall, my father shaves,
the water splashing like a fish
jumping every time
he swishes the razor through it.
In low tones, he speaks to my mother
and they close their bedroom door.
My sister sleeps. Awake,
I dream a journey I will one day take.

Platonic Sex

What a depressing idea of love, to make it a relation between two people, whose monotony must be vanquished as required by adding extra people.
    —*Gilles Deleuze and Claire Parnet, A Thousand Plateaus: Capitalism and Schizophrenia*

So this is intercourse—
you asking me by touch to say
yes, I'm game, I'm up for this
lifelong tapestry of ideas,

and me asking you through a smile
to pick up yesterday's thread
when you said I just learned from Yeats
how crosses and roses work together,

then you asking me by phone
what I meant about the difference
between passion and romance,
the middle path and mediocrity,

and we asking each other,
sitting in your cold car past midnight,
living and dead stars crossing and rising
over the whirling earth, to say perhaps,

to say that, if yes,
we would seek the others,
we would place ourselves
in the path of meteors.

Warm Spell in November

Yesterday, she left her voice
(usually pure water,
now flecked with sand)
on my answering machine.
"Just waking up," she said,
six hours away by plane.

I called her back last night.
She was in her queen-sized bed.
"Turning in early," she said,
trying to make up for sleep
lost at the conference here,
where we stayed up all night, talking.

I wondered what she was wearing,
but didn't ask, afraid
it would be far too easy to book myself
on the next flight to Seattle.

Friends ask me, "Why not go?
What's holding you back?"

I've never been one at carnivals
to pass up a rollercoaster,
or much else, for that matter,
but there's a loneliness in our voices
I don't trust.

No way we could make love right
and keep each other, so we turn over now
in half-empty beds on two coasts.

I bought turnips the other day—

do you know how to cook them?
It's been chilly for weeks
so I was primed for winter.
But now the wind has shifted to summer,
and I swear I can almost smell
cotton candy in the air.

Adam's Deposition

(Genesis 3: 1-12)

We would lie
naked in sunwarmth,
talking hour upon hour,
our slack language
sweet as honeysuckle
on an almost aimless breeze.
Or we would walk all afternoon,
through grasses, stopping
only to eat of the garden.

And then, one day, while I dozed,
happy just to know she was near,
she came to me, her mind different—
how can I put it?—humming
like bees in clover, ready
for something untasted.

I had never heard her so awake,
so full of purpose and wonder.
I wanted to go where she went,
and so yes, I said, let us both
put it into our mouths.

Where Your Mouth Is

She kisses, you say, the way a dog dreams:
a little somewhere else, a little wracked
by the cries that curve through her throat, surprised
by how red-hot real her feelings seem,
and though you like that she says your kisses transport her
beyond the realm of the living and the dead

to a kind of cloud, you allow, yes,
that you worry, that you wonder whether
you are on that cloud with her
or if she simply uses your body and mouth
to swing to a hideaway in memory, where
old loves wait to rendezvous.

My father once cautioned my old-fashioned mother
not to pose questions she wouldn't like the answers to,
which leads me to ask you this:
do you believe you're better off doing whatever
it takes to stay in the eye of her hurricane,
or would you risk ruin for the sake of the truth?

Woman Reading Billy Collins to the Blind

It's like most of the songs we sang in high school—
she, literally, doesn't know I exist
and, I suppose, outside the daydream
her smooth voice puts me in, she barely exists
for me. But she's reading, earnestly,
"Taking Off Emily Dickinson's Clothes"
and "Victoria's Secret," and soon she is my beloved,
for the first time in bed with me, and her care
with the rhythm of each line has become her hand
caressing my forehead, not in the mindless way
of the headboard bangers, but more
in the manner of the Madonna we imagine exists.

But this Madonna says "molded cups" and "more naked than
        ever,"
and I believe that, even if she has a husband
who makes her supremely happy, she still wants me
to know what intimacy with her is like.
So when she speaks to me of straps
falling away from shoulders and the relief
of a corset finally undone, I hear
incidental sounds in her reading
as if they were part of our making love:
her swallowing after a particularly long line
now the swallowing after prolonged, open-mouthed kissing,
and the gentle smoothing of a page just turned,
the arranging of sheet and blanket in the after-glow.

What would she think if she were now to read
my reading of her reading of these poems?
Perhaps as little or no better than a man
who buys a girl for fifteen minutes of pleasure
in a back room. But, no, she keeps on

speaking to me, so engaged now that she forgets
to say the page numbers, required
by the authorities of this textbook service for the blind,
causing a matron to open our door periodically
to insert "page 126 …
page 127," while she breezes on—
"camisole … sweetheart neck … undergarments,"
though I hear, for the first time, a weariness
in her voice, tinged with the remains of hope.
Has it been there all along?
What a fool I am, only hearing
the buzzing of my own desire, only thinking
of a carriage stopping by, too soon, for me.

Part Two

Farm Visit

After a long trip, we're settling in,
everyone but me congregating in the kitchen
where Grandma brews coffee and sets out pie.
The women catch up on family news;
Dad and Grandpa talk fishing.

In the living room, I skate across
the radio dial, past the Beatles and Beach Boys,
an all-news station from Philadelphia,
and talk shows on fluttery signals
from the midwest and deep south,
until I land on a hockey game from Fort Wayne.

From the kitchen, my brother
cranks up the volume of his car-ride complaint,
casts about for the barb that will bait Dad.
Boring parents, he says, and stupid hicks
are not the way he wants to spend his weekend.

Dishes rattle and coffee splashes
when Dad jumps up to smack my brother
back down into the platform rocker
which scrapes across linoleum
until it crashes into the cellar door.

I don't want to listen anymore.
I don't want to hear the scuffle
of an adolescent kicking wildly
or the smack of my father's palm on my brother's face.

I fiddle with the dial, touch the antenna
as if, by fishing among stars
for radio waves, I'll find a frequency
of magic that can set this household right.

Listening to New York Radio in the Middle of the Night

There, in Insomniac City
where the dial can easily hold
five languages beyond English
and stations bleed into each other,
Emily Dickinson—satisfied
she could no longer see to see—
spoke through a piano
while a Spanish man, half crying,
half singing, declared he too
would die if the one he most
desired did not give him
her undying love.
Between Emily and the Spanish man,
a sitar spoke harmoniously
about rock-steady faith,
while picking its way along
a path of dissonant doubt.
Commercial life finally
put to bed, Lennon
woke up from a good dream,
his imagination intact.
He sang with the sitar, calling
the chutney and raita left over
from last night's dinner to put on
spiritual livery.
They in turn inspired
the beans in my cabinet
to take on a holy presence,
and the cabinets themselves,
dazed at first, recalled
the distant spirits of trees.
And when the whole house became
tuned like this to the radio,

my father kindly caught
a coach from that other kingdom
to sit in my living room,
if only for a moment,
and casually talk with me
of ordinary life.

A Friend's Sudden Death

We were sitting in the kitchen
when my brother delivered the news.

His cat went on
cleaning herself.

Through a thin wall
his neighbors laughed.

I remember how deliberately
he poured the tea

and paused to inhale
its jasmine steam,

the way he ran his finger
around the rim of the cup.

Letter across the Border

Dear Brother,

I hope you aren't affronted by this letter,
opposed as you were to fictions about the soul and afterlife.
In my dream, where we talked in the car,
you were as believable as gravity and pain.

Who was it, then, who told me, "Going back
to the problem is the only way you'll solve it?"
I went back, and what had eluded me for hours,
revealed itself in a minute or two.

Some days, I walk down a hallway just to say
to myself, "I am walking. Look
how I put this foot in front, and then the other,"
and in saying that, I hear that my voice still works,
that I still have control over my lips and tongue.

We could do worse than to spend every moment of life
being fascinated with the nuts and bolts of living.
Are we any less fascinating in our dying, our unravelling?
You didn't seem to think so. Science was still science.

For a while, you could stand for fifteen minutes.
Washing the dishes, you said, made you feel normal.
Then dying moved you to the La-Z-Boy, then Grandma's chair
with the button to help you stand, then permanently to bed.

Your soul kept clapping its hands. Like Solzhenitsyn,
you composed poems in your head, but flat on your back
in your private gulag. You shouldn't have dissolved so soon.
That's what I think. But you would say it was just
a bad hand, which followed a slew of good ones.

There's winning and there's losing.
There's starting and then stopping.
Things work and then they don't.
It's nothing personal. It's not unfair.

Aunt Vivian

I didn't know which to wish for most
at our family reunions: her baked limas
or the chocolate cake with peanut butter icing.

In the nursing home, they lift her into a wheelchair
so we can go to the piano, where I play The Lord's Prayer
and How Great Thou Art, her favorites—
Ay aw, ay aw, all she can say.

I wonder if she means *Dave's gone, Dave's gone,*
commiserating with me about my brother.
Mom guesses *Jay's gone*—Aunt Vivian's husband.
My devout sister believes *Praise God, Praise God.*

I think of the crowd interpreting Jesus on the cross.
He wants wine ... He is calling Elijah.

My aunt's hands, those of the mixer and serving spoon,
rest in her silent lap. The days of cake are over.
Death now bakes itself into her bones.

What to Do When

When would it make sense, in your grief, for me to say, "The sun shines for you?" If not while your mother lies dying, then when? After one year? Two?

How long after my wife walks off with half my books and dinner plates should you let me pour from a carafe of sorrow before you burst in on me with a story you hope will make me laugh? When will I learn how to play wild and free with loss?

Every Sunday, at the cathedral organ, a man missing three fingers rattles souls and benches with Franck and Messiaen. Who told him, "Go ahead, give yourself over to them; they'll help you draw sunlight from your sacred hands?"

Captain Beth and My Guide Dog Yaeger

Kneeling on the door sill, she helps to lift
my squirming, aging guide across the threshold,
this dog I had to carry from the tarmac
up the rickety stairs into the plane.

I'd like to think she sees in him a colleague.
I'd like to picture her smiling as she finds out
he is named for a childhood hero of hers
who first thundered through the barrier of sound.

Maybe she'll invite him up with her
and they'll talk shop: responsibilities,
the joys of discipline, the ignorant trust of passengers.

She'll put the plane on automatic pilot
and they'll swap horror stories ("strictly off
the record.") And then, in the manner of mentors,
she will invite him to fly the plane.

"Forget the instrument panel," she will say.
"Obviously that's not for you. And the dog star,
forget that too. Just fly by the seat of your pants—
or follow your nose—however you guys say it."

But he will fold himself into a spot
beneath the seat, among the carry-ons,
knowing his rightful place, the job at hand.

Schoenberg

Why would a young dog
give itself to guide the blind?
Ask the right question
to get a useful answer.
Did the dog have a choice?

What did the dog do,
once they neutered it
and slammed the kennel door
on its freedom dream?
It did its best to flourish.

And what about you—what
choices do you have left?
Do you take pleasure,
as Schoenberg did in twelve tones,
unleashed by your limitations?

Capital Punishment

My dog,
innocent of crime,
died from a needle
that he jerked away from several times,
until it took two of them
to hold him still.

Before his heart stopped,
it beat wild drums of panic.
It didn't seem to make a difference
how often or how fervently we said
good night, relax, you'll be okay.
The fluorescent lights hummed.

Democracy

"Look at those eyes," she warbles,
as I settle myself and my guide
across from her on the bus.
"What kind of dog is that?"
I am about to answer
when a man farther back clears his throat
and says, "Yellow Labrador."
If he's going to speak for me,
at least he knows his breeds.
But he knows more than that—
he knows their innermost lives.
He says, "Saddest dogs in the world."
I wouldn't presume to know that,
but we live in a free country;
people can think what they want.
"Takes six years to train them."
He sounds like he enjoys
having tidbits of knowledge to share.
There's only one problem; he's wrong:
it's actually more like six months.
Fortunately for him,
we live in a democracy,
where opinion is equal to fact,
and we all have the right to vote.

Health Care

My mother asked her farmer brother to shoot the dog.
Cost effective, I guess—57.5 cents per mile
(standard government rate, taking into account
"wear and tear" on the car), times 20 miles
to the nearest vet, who may well be out, anyway,
tending to large, cash-producing animals.
Then there's the wasted time to factor in.
What difference could it make to a decaying dog,
flies buzzing at the stink, how its misery should end?

Even if she weren't your dog, common compassion
might have called you to kneel down and pet her first,
perhaps say a prayer, apologize.
At some point, though, you'd have to draw a line,
back off to put some distance between you
because, after all, there's no practical way
to say goodbye to those velvet ears with one hand
while shooting her between the eyes with the other.

After Reading Psalm 22

I am poured out like water;
all my bones are out of joint;
my heart within my breast is melting wax.
My mouth is dried out like a potsherd;
my tongue sticks to the roof of my mouth;
and you have laid me in the dust of the grave.
Packs of dogs close me in,
and gangs of evildoers circle round me;
they pierce my hands and my feet;
I can count all my bones.
—Psalm 22: 14-16

Yes, I say to the psalmist,
I know that dry-mouth terror.

My wet-mouthed dog, who lies on his bed
licking himself, might have, in another life,
as easily joined a circle of wolves
eager to rend my flesh, disjoint my bones.

How do we, the weak, live with fear,
knowing the hyena picks off stragglers?

I applaud those who dread
the thing they must do and still do it.

What is courage—
simple subtraction:
principle minus terror?

Or elementary addition:
good reflexes plus stupidity?

Make friends with your executioner, some say.
Give him something to think about.

Is courage refusing
to make it easy for a firing squad,
moving as much as you can,
or is it standing still?

As they drag me to the gallows,
will I shit my pants, or will I sing?

Coffee Shop

The cashier rang up a customer
then pointed to her newspaper.
"You read about the kid killed
in his own driveway last night?"
The woman backed out:
"There's nothing you can say," she said.

He kept talking, now to the closed door:
"Except that God works in fucked-up ways.
How else can you explain
a six-year-old crushed by a car
in front of his sister?
Fucked up, that's all you can say."

I stopped stirring my tea.
Why would anyone want a God
who would let that happen, I asked myself,
or worse, who would ordain it?
Why don't we just say
the idea of a God is fucked?
Let's just accept, said Nietzsche,
that we are here on our own.
Let's just face, said Feuerbach,
that God's a dead metaphor.

"It broke those first responders," the cashier said.
"They had to hose that boy off the driveway."
I'd scrub out any notion of God, but then
what should I do with the horse, the rose, the thrush,
the bristle-cone pine? Tell me, what should I do
with the guys who power-washed the drive?

Part Three

Complaint

In Sunday school, they told us if we prayed
and listened hard enough, you'd bend down low
to whisper in our ears. And if we read
the words that other people heard you say
from a mountain top or deep in the desert,
and believed them the way a dog believes
his master will eventually come home,
or studied them longer than most dogs live,
you'd tell us, in time, what we needed to know.

You bless my table and you bless my bed.
You are math and physics; you star in your own great show.
I do not take these things for granted, God.
At meals, I offer thanks. Inside my wife,
I call your name. But you never talk to me.
You merely send me gifts, albeit great ones,
like a traveling father too busy catching planes.

Men of Fire

I have lived with men of fire,
men with smoky eyes who, early on,
learned the art of swallowing flames
and who now, in the space of a spark,
will call them back,
men who have smouldered on couches,
fumed in bed,
and scorched the backsides
of their children with switches.

Perhaps because of this,
some imbalance of elements,
I am always heading
for the water in you,
willing to travel
any distance
for the scent of moss
and rain-soaked earth.
But because I will drown in water,
you must let me,
make me,
come up for air.

Holy Mystery

"He's just a friend," she says. I know she's lying.
When I stop by, conflicting stories from her housemates
tell me that—she's out, no, she's in
but can't come down. Later, frozen noise
behind a bedroom door confirms the worst.
A week off campus and I've missed a lot
more than history. Laws of the universe have changed.

After dinner I return with vesper prayers.
"Stay with me," I say, "for it is evening,
and the day is almost over." But his prayers
have reached her first, so she has plans.
On the bed where she first gave herself to me
I sit and cry while she dresses for her date.

She walks me to the chapel (the only place
I know to go) and leaves me at the organ
(the only thing I know to do). But what
I want to do is touch her breast beneath
her half-unbuttoned shirt the way I did
that hottest of spring nights a year ago
when we sat in the transept leafing through
the hymnal for some half-remembered verse.

I bite my lip and push on from a prelude
to a fugue until the notes dissolve in chaos
and I slap the keys the way my sister used to,
slam the organ shut, and careen out the door.
My body weaves along the sidewalk like
a party-goer's car at 2 a.m.

A woman calls my name and takes my hand.
She leads me to her room, where, for an hour,
I ramble like a man on too much wine.

This outspoken Christian housemate of my girlfriend,
known to most for justice more than mercy,
never says a word about my soul
or asks me questions I don't want to answer.

When she walks me to her door and says she'll pray
for me, I want to hold her. I don't know what
makes me think she'll let me do it, and I don't
know why when I reach for her, the night all quiet
except for crickets and some far-off music,
she draws me in and reverently lets her lips,
firm and gentle as a chalice, touch my own.

Easter, 2000

Jesus is as odd to me
as a cell phone would have been
to someone in 1900,
and the resurrection as incredible as a call
coming into the back seat of a van
where someone listens to a CD playing oldies.

In 1800, he is the car itself,
and long before that, his ascension what the paved road
would have been to the Neanderthal.

Mary with your breasts full of milk,
Martha with your lap of life and honey,
where did you come from
but spots of wetness?

Joseph, the sap runs fast in you,
like the electricity of ideas
we each circulate
without knowing how.

The idea of death—
does it confound you, too?

Oh, sweet Magdalene, come!
Lead me through the teeming world,
past all obstacles to holy mystery.

Make me into a human antenna,
fill me with impulses for language,
wash me in the mother tongue
and play your best songs in my blood.

I have always wanted to walk in faith.
Marry me to the outside;

marry me to the inside.
Place my palms on the handlebars of the sun
and set my feet on the stones of the cold stream
that flows down to the river in the canyon.

Dolly

You think you should prepare yourself
for a good deed
you've been meaning to do for months
with a hammer and nails
you haven't yet bought.

But first, you have a suitcase of letters
it's time to send,
so you walk along Lender's Avenue,
turn right past the access road,
and let yourself into the copy center
that doubles as post office annex.

Rose or Jo-Ellen will handle the letters,
but it's Dolly you watch
in the rear left corner,
her face that of a peasant
who has just set down
a bucket of blackberries
she'll bake in a pie.

She hasn't been waiting for you in particular.

She turns in her light cotton dress brimming over
with fresh cream, turns toward machines that splash wild ink
and thump a rhythm your headboard once knew.

Let them mail out all your desire
and see if they'll keep your suitcase
behind the counter until the day you return.
Then go from here to the abandoned cathedral
and walk the Stations of the Cross alone.
Feel how dry your mouth has become.
Try not to think about blackberry pie.

Another Day

You are watching television—
something about your breath,
how bad it is,
your crotch,
until it makes you want to scratch.
Armpits, hair, feet, gut, skin—
nothing is secret.

Well, you think, I don't know
who they're talking to. Not me.
And you go out
to your little shed
to rearrange the way
the tools hang and fiddle
with the coping saw, and then
you do some other things
like going to the grocery store
where you try not to think
too much about gingivitis
while you select apples.

That night, your wife holds you
briefly before rolling over,
putting half the mattress between you.
It feels like a moment less
than the night before, which was
a whisper less than last week,
but it might be your imagination. Nothing
personal, you say. She has
a lot on her mind from work, and besides,
it's ten years of marriage.

She's already asleep,
little puffing sounds

coming from her mouth
on every downbreath.
Three cars and how many
electric bills
since you first slept together?
You lie still,
barely breathing,
not turning over,
afraid to wake her
by jostling the bed.

You think of something new
like ballroom dancing,
(can that actually work?)
something old, like
long car trips together
and worrying she
might be pregnant.

You back out of the covers,
holding your breath,
and feel your way
downstairs to the stereo,
but you can't think
of what you want
to hear, so you sit
with the headphones on
and nothing playing,
rocking in the rocking chair
while the refrigerator
cycles on and off.

Moving Out

From the family room, a man hands out box after box,
his half of their dishes, records and books,
to friends who are helping him leave his wife.
He will miss the way she nurtures each rose
in her garden, the way she caresses the keys
of her piano, the way she loves this house.

But he can no longer live in this house
which confines him increasingly like the locked metal box
made for Houdini—no exit, no keys.
He has searched for an answer in therapy and books,
one that would bloom overnight like a rose,
one that would free him to stay with his wife.

He was not a bad husband, nor she a bad wife.
They were just two college kids with the dream of a house,
maybe a little girl (they could call her Rose),
perhaps a big picture window with a flower box,
and a cozy library for all of their books.
To have a house of their own with two sets of keys

seemed like the path to maturity, as if having those keys
could unlock the secrets of being husband and wife,
things only guessed at from reading books
about a hero and heroine with a castle for a house.
Their disappointment leaked from some Pandora's box
in their hearts, swelling in volume until it rose

to blot out the beauty of each blood-red rose
and muffle the music from the ivory keys.
The man went to the gym to work out and box,
hoping to reduce tension between him and his wife.
She tried cooking fancy meals, redecorating the house,
and buying him records and gadgets and books.

When all seemed in vain, they balanced their checkbooks
and stayed up nights talking until the sun rose
about where they'd gone wrong, who'd get the house,
and the fun on their honeymoon in the Florida Keys.
They cried about not being husband and wife
and how the house, for the man, had turned into a box.

Now, box by box, he is closing the books
on this life with the wife who loves the rose,
this life handed over with his keys to the house.

Scrapbook of an Unsuccessful Marriage

the idea
that some people
position stereo speakers
based on appearance

nocturns on a baby grand downstairs
while I read myself to sleep

a refusal to laugh
at my mean jokes

she watching movies of husbands
plotting to murder their wives
while I read Nancy Friday
on men's sexual fantasies

James Herriot read aloud
in an average diner
with great cheeseburgers
in rural New York
on the way to Montreal

Montreal

slammed doors
a slap in the face

a car accident
in the rain
between the Bach Magnificat
and ice cream with friends

someone to love
in a hospital

our unspoken worry
that I could not love
through adversity

she insisting that the accident
was her fault
no matter how easy
the white cop made it
for her to pin it
on the black man

the grief I got
for not wiping off
the tea kettle
every night

how to make
a pie crust

fear of raw eggs
so that I don't lick
the beaters anymore

Episcopal propriety
monopoly on a picnic table
premarital sex with a Christian

my first taste of Mexican food
a second look at Jane Austen
one third of her life

Divorce

Tonight, it was a clock
falling off the wall,
completely unprovoked.

Perhaps you'd like to tell me
there are ghosts in my house.

Okay, tell me.

Or that strange convections
traveling from my bathroom window
(the only one open)
conspired to knock it off.

Tell me an old nail
having stayed in place
for five years
gave out,

or the wall
tired of this thorn in the flesh
just let go.

Tell me that, before they knew it,
they came to a resolution
in the middle of the night

with no one there to stop them,
no one to fix anything.

Winter Walks

Some strange man
has moved into my house,
signed on to a dream
where I signed off.
His underwear now tumbles with hers in the dryer.
They lie in front of what used to be our hearth.

I wander the streets, poised
between loneliness and possibility.

Some days I think
I will quit it all,
but then a woman
admires my long fingers,
or, reading while walking,
collides with me,
and we laugh.

So I go on,
sniffing for the scent of contentment:
smoke from a fireplace,
perfumed dryer exhaust,
fried chicken from a kitchen fan.

Yet, I am ready
to turn the corner,
meet no one,
and go back to my apartment
to cook when I feel like it
and play Louis Armstrong
until the sun crests the hill.

Old Records

Alone, and seeking
a diversion, I choose
a record that, in high school,
kept me calm—
some days, almost inspired.

I put it on
to parse its hidden meaning
like reading recipes
to catalog ingredients
of desserts I used to crave.

But now, the crashing chords
and pseudo-classical sound,
poetic lines that overshoot
their mark, embarrass me
and trail off in hollowness.

Amused and puzzled,
sorry I have played it,
I let it finish,
then put it on the shelf.
I think about a woman
I once loved.

Calling Allen Ginsberg

"We're not our skin of grime," you said
and I thought of Blake once talking to you and you now talking
    to me,
you who once found Walt Whitman in the grocery store and
    implored him among the pork chops.
Now, I have questions of my own.
What must we do to sing? Wait till the room closes in and the
    sky squeezes down?
Make love with someone who will steal our favorite jazz
    records and phonograph?
Deliver ourselves into the corporate cage to pay for precious
    books—
books sold off by parasites for drug money?
Can you teach me, a straight, middle-class goy
with a mostly happy life and no mother in an asylum,
about howling and holiness, the weight of love, the poet's
    knowledge of nakedness,
and sunflowers? Especially sunflowers.

Living with Others

Last night as I was leaving,
Animal Control was just arriving
to collect the squirrel from the baited trap.
Eight now in two weeks.

While I'm sleeping, showering, listening to Brahms,
they're up there gnawing, chasing, crying
in what sounds like sexy pleasure.
I don't know where they're coming in,
or how they're getting out.

I had a wife once, and some days
she chewed her way through my exterior.
On others, I flung the door wide open.

Maybe I should just return the cage,
learn to live with rodents
who, after all, only want to do
the things we say we honor:
make a stable home, raise their young.

But this is all wrong;
ex-wives and squirrels are not the same.
Still, last time, the wires that got crossed,
the burning,
the length of silence afterward.

What the Mice Taught Me

I liked it best when they died in the Havahart traps—
none of the futility and sham of releasing them
outside with the certainty they'd come back in,
but no outright killing, either.

An unfortunate oversight, I told myself,
having forgotten to check the traps for days,
though I never truly forgot them. I just didn't
make a habit of putting them on my to-do list.

One day, I'd had enough: their shit on my food,
their urine. I bought the expensive model
with a patented backbreaker.
For a while, I had to use ear plugs.
Now the snap is one more house noise—like the dryer buzzing,
that kick from the pipes when the toilet stops.

I can't imagine killing a man.
I can't even imagine hurting a dog or a cat.
Yet, when an old love called me long-distance
from her lonely life in Allentown,
though I can't quite say that the lying was easy at first,
it was easier than I would have thought it should have been.
I listened, rapt, to her sad story, adding
a few random resentments of my own,
and even though I didn't know her husband,
I figured that he probably had it coming.

Part Four

At Lunch

Her thin arms rest upon the table.
I felt them once;

it seems like many times.
Her arms are light

as the French pastry
we order for dessert.

Sometimes, when she laughs,
everything seems too bright.

But I would not want her to stop.
I worry someone will open

all the windows in this room
and she will float out

through the screens.
Against that possibility,

I ask her to read to me:
Sonnets from the Portuguese.

I want her to leave
her indelible scent in the ink.

When He Knew They'd Never Marry

She tells him she would love to come for dinner,
but wants to shower first, after running.
He hangs up the phone. He thinks:
coconut shampoo. He imagines tasting
the water that sluices between her breasts.

Only a week before, his grandmother lay in stainless steel,
draped in velvet covers, her skin waxy and cold.

When his girlfriend arrives, he tells her how
someday he hopes to find out what it's like
before she showers. "Pretty ripe," she says.
"I don't think you'd want to."

He waited with the other pallbearers while
the undertaker removed roses and jewelry
from the coffin, lowered the lid with a soft thump,
and vacuum-sealed it with a crank.
No sound, no smell, no nothing, he thought.

"No," he protests. "It would be so hot.
I'd like to open your clothes hamper and inhale,
to bury my face in the armpits of your dress,
in the crotch of your underwear."
His girlfriend cringes and turns away.
"You're disgusting," she says.

The ground was dry, the water table low.
Flowers spilling out of several baskets
had little scent beside the open grave.

Small Scene, Minor Characters

Yesterday,
teaching tenth grade,
looking for a way
to let Shakespeare speak again,
I said, "Let's choose groups
to perform scenes from Caesar."

Christine, absent then,
has no place to go, and no group
seems eager to take her in.

"I'm just going to cry," she says,
putting her head down
on the backs of her hands,
her silken hair falling
over the bevelled edges of her desk
to light upon her lap.

"Come on, you diva," I laugh,
"save the drama for Shakespeare."
Whistling, I scooch and zigzag
her desk across the room
to bump up against the others.

But her head is still down,
and it is only then
I hear the first sob,
feel the shoulders shake.
"My grandfather. My grandfather
died on Monday. I saw him
Sunday, but he was asleep.
He was waiting for my sister
to get back home.
She did on Monday,

and then he died,
and I didn't get to talk to him."

We sit and listen to her soliloquy:
Cinna, three Plebeians and a teacher,
her partners in Act III, Scene 3,
now no more willing to start without her
than my aunts to unpack their picnic baskets
before everyone's arrived.

I offer to get her Kleenex.
I come back with toilet paper.
"That's fine," she says, "I'll be alright,"
and wiping off her glasses
laughs at how the salty tears
make her lenses look.

"Does anyone know," she asks,
"if Cinna had granddaughters?
Is there any way
we can find that out?"

To a Young Girl Watching Television

Your body is already good enough,
although the TV ads will not say so.
Don't let them talk you into buying stuff.

They claim without their rouge and powder puff
you won't find love; they don't want you to know
your body is already good enough.

Your chest's too small, they say, your hands too rough,
your hair too dull, and on and on they go.
Don't let them talk you into buying stuff.

The way you climb a tree, your muscles tough
as Tide on dirt, will more than amply show
your body is already good enough.

The men who sell these ads live on a bluff
of loneliness where money's all they know.
Don't let them talk you into buying stuff.

With legs unshaved and skin untanned rebuff
the lies which make you pay some C.E.O.
Your body is already good enough.
Don't let them talk you into buying stuff.

How to Live Well
(a few guesses)

If you have the choice to sit
squarely in the middle of a cushion
or to straddle the crack between two,
pick the middle of one,
but in important matters, don't
set too much store in comfort.
Don't turn on the television
unless you've planned to watch
something particular for days,
and it's still as appetizing
as the smell of Thanksgiving
when you first step into your mother's house.
Sit and do nothing.
Do everything you can.
Don't cry as a way out of taking action.
Don't act as a way out of crying.
Don't confuse bravado with bravery,
or fear with a shortage of courage.
Lay down a line of thought, and then oppose it.
Acquire three heartbreaking mistakes
sooner rather than later;
they'll teach you how to be tough
and compassionate at the same time.
Read widely and often.
Cut yourself at least as many breaks
as you would someone desperately flawed in a novel.
Don't let yourself off the hook
as quickly as you're tempted to.
Tear up this list.

Providence

I met my girlfriend in yoga.
I was there on a whim.
Her class across town had been canceled.
"Meant to be," she laughed, six months later.
"Dumb luck," I said.

When the tsunami struck,
Thomas Goodpenny crossed himself
and thanked God for his charmed life—
the deal he was supposed to close in Sri Lanka
had already fallen through.

Finally, when pushed to the wall,
my mother admitted, "No,
I don't absolutely know
there's a heaven—nobody does—
but I don't want to take the chance by not believing."

I just shuffle the options:
take my dog in the car
and hope there's no accident,
or leave her at home
and pray for no fire.

Yet, last week at a writers' workshop,
the leader dumped a pile of cookie fortunes
in front of my girlfriend. "Take one," he said,
"and see if it doesn't somehow surprise your poem."
"Wait till you hear this, Mr. Dumb-Luck,"
she whispered to me, tucking it into her pocket.
Back in her room she unfolded it:
"Stop searching forever; happiness is right next to you."
I thought she meant it for me.
She thought it was meant for her.

Door

You had a boyfriend,
and I had my own untangling to do,
so we talked on the phone as friends,
compressing years of history into hours.
Yes, you said, your marriage never ran right
but you love the son it brought you.
Your only regret: the daughter it never gave.
"I wanted a girl too," I couldn't help saying,
and soon, we'd named her. She had a name.

"Hold it, hold it," I broke in.
"Isn't this where we need to slam the door?"
"Do we have to slam it?" you wanted to know.
I asked if there was a latch and, if so, how strong.
"There is," you said, "and it's strong,
but some days get awfully windy."

Love Note

Yes, we have no bananas.
(from a popular song of 1923)

You are gone, but the house is still full of you:
the soft sculpture of the sheet and blanket
just as you left it,
your forgotten cell phone on my nightstand,
the round aroma of the soup you made yesterday
still hovering in the corners of my upstairs office
where I am writing this.

I thought I had no more poems in me today
than the most famous song about bananas has bananas. And
maybe I still don't. But I have
a blind man's pictures, memories in every other sense.
Maybe even the sound of your breathing, if I'm quiet enough.
Maybe even the taste of you, a faint secret in my mouth.

Why I'm Crazy about Her

Because I can tell when she's blushing over the phone
Because she chair-dances and talks with her hands while she's
    driving
Because she unzips my ski jacket to get in closer
Because she licks potato chips thoroughly before she eats them
And yet kissing her feels more like conversation than foreplay
(Is it finally time to give up the bachelor life?)
Because she'd charge into a hornet's nest while I hung back
Because she throws her wet hair over me after she gets out of
    the shower
And reads a hot poem on my voicemail every thirty days
Because once, after a movie, she said,
"Look at us, sitting here bawling our hearts out,
and we couldn't be happier."

Tonight, When I Talk to My Guide Dog

"Chandler," I say, "maybe I should marry you."
Everywhere—in airports, meetings and restaurants,
at bus stops and on street corners—
people feel compelled to tell me,
"He looks up to you with such love."

People and their weird projections.
He nuzzles a bone to stall for time.
"Naw," he says, "that would ruin everything.
Besides, she's good for you. You've been a block dog long
     enough,
charming women for scraps and a warm place to stay—
and a little commitment wouldn't hurt you any."

I'm about to issue the Quiet command,
when he bounces up and bangs his nose on my knee.
"Come on," he says, "I've got to go out."
As I snap on his leash, he gives his head a shake.
"You know," he says, "you might even grow to like it."

The Next Day

It took her
leaving for work
before I could
open the fist
my heart had become
enough to let
the cool air
of reflection
blow across my
hot resistance.

Wandering around
her apartment
before catching
a bus home
I saw how
her things could
call me back
to love her,
how I wouldn't
want anyone
to ruin even
the least of them.

I wouldn't want
her to lose
any more than
I'd already taken—
wouldn't want
not to turn the key
for the second lock
and check them both
a second time.

Questions

It was you, Darling,
oh it was most definitely you.
Even in a dream, I know
the exact angle of our noses in kissing.
I know the fragrant melange
of fish and flower that is
your olfactory fingerprint
in the nakedness of love.

So it was strange, then,
that you were my sister in this dream,
this dream where we giggled and worried that our father
might innocently, imprudently, peek in.

Not my sister, to be precise,
but in the role of sister.
I've been asking myself all day, why.
Why with all the wanting,
no reduction in our usual desire,
would you be made a sister?
To send me back to my real sister
with better than I've given her before?
To show me what long-time lived-in love looks like?

And what if we all had sisters
who would fall asleep with us?
Would we learn earlier to love?

Come, my Love,
isn't it time we were family?

Double Concerto

The piano's notes ring clean as this morning's air,
then the solo flute, Wisdom herself, and the strings
enfold the world in warm arms, saying,
"This, too, shall pass—the heartache, the ecstasy,
everything—and through it all, you will be okay."
It was for this that I fell in love with music,
for this that I scoured the stores each week for records
of intimate conversations and public professions.
And yet, there is no music here with us
inside this sleeping bag except, far off,
an early mourning dove and the gentle rocking
of a lake with which we harmonize, a viola
and a horn, in this, the true music, even at this late date,
for which composers and players helped me wait.

Why We Need New Year's Day and the Passage of Seasons

Because we are iron in a smithy world
which heats and hammers us beyond self-recognition,
leaving us slow to learn renewal,
too grumpy or fogged most mornings
to notice that our hearts still surge blood
to every point along the body's map,
and that our minds are still what computers emulate.

After all, even monks with no other life
cannot harness themselves to awareness every second.
And yet, a garbage collector I know
carries his life like a diamond,
and an exhausted mother
immersed in four-child babble all day
hitches her mind to a book each night,
if only for five minutes,
before she careens into sleep.

Praise, then, to the policeman who paints portraits
and to the bank teller who keeps a journal.
Praise to the thwarted shop steward who keeps
his standing appointment to play catch with his child.
Praise to the heartbroken social worker who subscribes to the
        symphony.
Praise to the math teacher who photographs birds
and to the roofer who, hoping for hope,
believes that next year his team will do better.

Praise the toddler and the hospice-dweller
as they stumble in new passages.
Praise all who breathe.
Praise all who once breathed and now nourish the ground.
Praise all whose stories have already been written

and all those who still have at least one more chance.
(Seventy times seven, says Jesus,
are the chances we each should have.)

Let the fireman remember his own life as he chops with the
    axe.
Let neither the minister neglect his wife,
nor the doctor her husband.
Let none of us simply swallow our lives whole.
But if the minister, the doctor, and we should fail,
let us have new years and fresh seasons.
Let us have seventy times seven chances.

Acknowledgements

Many thanks to the magazines where some of these poems first appeared:

Atlanta Review: "Double Concerto"
Hampden-Sydney Poetry Review: "Winter Walks"
The Louisville Review: "Night Journey"
The New York Times: "Democracy"
Nine Mile Magazine: "Captain Beth and My Guide Dog Yaeger," "Listening to New York Radio in the Middle of the Night," "My Pants Are Drenched with Rain," "Platonic Sex," "Tonight, When I Talk to My Guide Dog," "What the Mice Taught Me"
One Art: "Farm Visit," "Schoenberg," "Why We Need New Year's Day and the Passage of Seasons"
Prairie Schooner: "Some Holy Saturday"
Present Time: "To a Young Girl Watching Television"
Schuylkill Valley Journal: "Coffee Shop," "Dolly," "How to Live Well," "Living with Others," "Men of Fire," "What to Do When"
Wordgathering: "A Blind Boy's First Glimpse of Heaven," "American Girl and French Boy Take a Walk," "Love Note," "Measuring Distance," "Moving Out," "We All Have Something of the Poet in Us"

"A Blind Boy's First Glimpse of Heaven" appeared in *School for the Blind* by Daniel Simpson, published by Poets Wear Prada, Hoboken, New Jersey, in 2014.
"A Blind Boy's First Glimpse of Heaven," "Listening to New York Radio in the Middle of the Night," "My Pants Are Drenched with Rain," "Adam's Deposition," "Providence," and "Questions" appeared in *Border Songs: A Conversation in Poems* by Ona Gritz and Daniel Simpson, published by Finishing Line Press, Georgetown, Kentucky, in 2017.

Many thanks to Molly Fisk who taught me how fun revision can be and who reminded me to be compassionate toward myself while being exacting with my poems. She has the rare gift of making one's poems better without making them in her image.

I want to express my deep appreciation to Ona Gritz, Alina Macneal, Nina Schafer, and Dave Worrell, fellow members of the Lansdowne Station Writers Group, for their uncanny ability to walk around my poems and find windows where I thought I had created doors and doors where I thought I had created windows.

Additional heartfelt thanks to Ona Gritz for her sustaining belief in me and for her invaluable feedback throughout all phases of this book.

About the Author

Daniel Simpson was born in Williamsport, Pennsylvania, in 1952. After attending the Overbrook School for the Blind through eighth grade, Simpson became one of the first blind students in the Philadelphia area to go to a public school. He earned a Bachelor of Arts in English and music from Muhlenberg College, where he graduated *summa cum laude* and Class Salutatorian. After receiving a Master of Music degree in organ performance from Westminster Choir College, where he had the opportunity to sing with major symphony orchestras, Simpson traveled to Paris for a year of private study with the world-renowned, blind organist, Andre Marchal.

Upon returning to the U.S., he worked as a church musician, computer programmer, and high school English teacher, earning a Master of Arts in English and a teaching certificate from the University of Pennsylvania along the way. Between 2002 and 2015, he served as Access Technology Consultant to the Free Library of Philadelphia and the Philadelphia Library for the Blind. He has worked as a technical support specialist for BARD, the Library of Congress's braille and audio book download service for the print-impaired, since 2010.

"Let's Walk Together," a composition for bass soloist and choir, based on a text written by Simpson, received its premiere performance by Voces8 in London in December, 2020. Voces8 and four other choirs also performed "A Song Everyone Can Sing," for which he served as lyricist in March, 2019. In 2017, he and his wife, Ona Gritz, collaborated on two books, as co-authors of *Border Songs: A Conversation in Poems* and as co-editors of *More Challenges for the Delusional*, an anthology of prose, poetry, and prompts. *School for the Blind*, his first collection of poems, came out in 2014. His work has been anthologized in *About Us: Essays from the Disability Series of the New York Times, Welcome to the Resistance: Poetry as*

Protest, and *Beauty Is a Verb: The New Poetry of Disability,* and has appeared in *Prairie Schooner, The Cortland Review,* and many other journals.

The recipient of a Fellowship in Literature from the Pennsylvania Council on the Arts, Simpson has been invited to read his poetry at the Dodge Poetry Festival, the Free Library of Philadelphia, Philadelphia's First Person Arts, and at the Cornelia Street Cafe in New York City. He has appeared at World Cafe Live, Philadelphia, on WHYY-FM's Radio Times with Marty Moss-Coane, and on Public Radio International's The Upside of Down with Dan Ariely. Simpson has been singing with the Mendelssohn Chorus of Philadelphia, a 120-voice choir, for more than 25 years. His blog and links to his work can be found at insidetheinvisible.wordpress.com.

Made in United States
North Haven, CT
01 February 2023

31930671R00059